UNFORGE CHRISTMAS EXPERIENCE IN LONDON 2024-2025

MW01601942

TABLE OF CONTENTS

CHAPTER 1

INTRODUCTION TO A LONDON CHRISTMAS

London at Christmas is a magical experience like no other. Each December, the city transforms into a glowing wonderland, blending the rich traditions of the past with vibrant, modern-day festivities. The energy is almost tangible—streets are adorned with glistening lights, shop windows are dressed with intricate holiday displays, and a feeling of warmth permeates every corner despite the crisp winter air. London's Christmas season is not merely about decorations or even gifts; it's a celebration of togetherness, tradition, and a hearty embrace of the season's joy. Whether you're a first-time visitor or a seasoned traveler, discovering Christmas in London promises to feel like stepping into a storybook, filled with one-of-a-kind experiences that will make you fall in love with the city's holiday spirit.

In London, Christmas holds a special magic that weaves together history, tradition, and modern sparkle. While each city has its holiday charm, London stands out because of the distinct character that each borough brings to the festivities. Iconic landmarks like the Tower of London, Big Ben, and the Thames take on a new life, beautifully illuminated and infused with the warmth of holiday cheer. There's a certain vibrancy to London at Christmas that makes even routine sights—like double-decker buses and bustling street crossings—feel like part of a festive backdrop.

The city's holiday magic isn't just confined to its sights. Londoners go all out to celebrate, hosting events that bring together communities, friends, and families. Outdoor markets spring up across the city, filling the streets with scents of roasted chestnuts, mulled wine, and freshly baked treats, while local choirs sing carols that echo through the busy lanes. And while London may be a fast-paced city, the holiday season brings a kind of softness; people take time to appreciate each other's company, share festive greetings with strangers, and revel in the seasonal spirit that unites them all.

Planning a trip to London during Christmas requires a little preparation, but it's well worth the effort. December in London is a bustling season, with attractions filled with locals and visitors alike who want to experience the holiday cheer. The winter temperatures here can vary from chilly to downright frosty, so packing layers is essential. Think warm coats, scarves, gloves, and sturdy footwear; London is a walkable city, and the best parts of it are often best discovered on foot. Yet, there's a coziness to the cold—it brings with it a natural invitation to explore warm cafés, indulge in a hot cocoa, or relax by a fireplace in one of the city's historic pubs.

It's also wise to plan around London's holiday calendar, as certain events and attractions can be especially crowded, while others may close on specific days. The days leading up to Christmas and New Year's Eve are especially lively, with Christmas Eve, Christmas Day, and Boxing Day each having their own unique traditions. Knowing these dates allows you to pace your sightseeing, ensuring you can experience the holiday events you most want to attend. With a little foresight, you'll be able to soak up London's holiday spirit without the overwhelm of peak crowds.

In addition, it's essential to book your accommodations and tickets for popular attractions early. From cozy boutique hotels to grand, luxurious accommodations, London offers a wide range of options, but demand is high in December. Finding a place to stay close to the heart of the festivities—be it near Trafalgar Square, Covent Garden, or the South Bank—means you'll always be just a short stroll from London's Christmas wonder.

With London as your festive playground, this chapter sets the tone for what promises to be an unforgettable Christmas experience. The city awaits with open arms, ready to share

its unique blend of holiday traditions, cozy comforts, and boundless seasonal cheer. In the chapters that follow, we'll dive deeper into each facet of London's Christmas magic, offering tips, hidden gems, and all the insight you need to truly make the most of your time here.

1.1 THE MAGIC OF CHRISTMAS IN LONDON

There's something truly extraordinary about Christmas in London. The city transforms each December, embracing a holiday spirit that's hard to capture anywhere else in the world. For weeks, the streets are bathed in twinkling lights, with iconic neighborhoods like Oxford Street, Regent Street, and Covent Garden adorned with glittering decorations that elevate even a simple stroll into a breathtaking experience. But beyond the lights and décor, there's a richness to London's Christmas traditions that give the season here a distinct character.

Each corner of the city carries its own piece of festive charm. Historic buildings, from Westminster Abbey to St. Paul's Cathedral, hold special holiday services that bring people together in a moving display of togetherness and reflection. Traditional carol singing fills the air, echoing through these storied landmarks and creating a sense of connection to London's past. Then there's Trafalgar Square, where a towering Christmas tree—gifted from Norway as a thank-you for British support during World War II—stands tall and elegantly lit, becoming a gathering spot for people of all backgrounds.

London's holiday season doesn't just cater to nostalgia; it also offers modern holiday twists that are both exciting and unforgettable. Festive markets pop up in places like Southbank and Leicester Square, each with its own distinct character, offering handmade crafts, festive foods, and warming cups of mulled wine. Meanwhile, Hyde Park's Winter Wonderland brings the excitement of an amusement park, complete with ice skating, thrilling rides, and bustling food stalls that beckon families and friends to celebrate in the open winter air. With every turn, London's festivities offer something new to discover, blending tradition and innovation in a way that only this city can.

But perhaps what makes Christmas in London so enchanting is the atmosphere itself. From the crispness of the air to the glow of lanterns in cozy pubs, there's an energy that makes the city feel alive with seasonal cheer. Even on cold winter evenings, people gather in markets and squares, wrapped in scarves and laughter, savoring the chance to celebrate together. London at Christmas isn't just about what you see—it's about what you feel. It's a place where the hustle and bustle of everyday life pauses, and for a moment, everyone is invited to step into a season filled with warmth, joy, and a sense of magic.

1.2

PREPARING FOR A WINTER GETAWAY

If you're planning a December visit to London, it's wise to come prepared. Winter here brings chilly, sometimes wet weather, with temperatures averaging between 2°C and 8°C (36°F to 46°F). But don't let the cold deter you—the city's beauty shines brightly even under grey skies, and there's a distinct coziness to exploring its festive wonders wrapped in winter layers. With the right packing list and a bit of planning, you'll be ready to enjoy London's Christmas magic in comfort.

When packing, think layers. London's weather can be unpredictable, often shifting from cold to colder within a day. Bring warm essentials: a good coat, scarves, gloves, and a hat are must-haves to keep the chill at bay. Comfortable, waterproof shoes are key, as London is best explored by foot, and the holiday markets and light displays demand a good amount of walking. If you're planning to ice skate or visit open-air markets, extra warmth—like thermal socks or an extra jumper—can make a big difference in your comfort.

Beyond clothing, be mindful of London's holiday schedule. Christmas Eve, Christmas Day, and Boxing Day (December 26) hold special significance, with many businesses, public transport services, and attractions operating on reduced hours or closing altogether. Christmas Day itself sees an almost magical pause: the usually bustling city streets are peaceful and quiet as families gather, creating a rare and beautiful scene in this lively metropolis. Knowing this in advance allows you to plan your outings around these closures and make the most of the holiday festivities.

It's also wise to book in advance for popular activities. Christmas theater shows, from the enchanting *Nutcracker* ballet to pantomimes filled with laughter, are in high demand, and festive dining experiences often fill up quickly. Many of London's famous restaurants and hotels offer special Christmas menus that provide an authentic taste of British holiday fare—roasted meats, stuffing, and all the trimmings. Booking ahead not only guarantees your spot but also enhances the anticipation of an unforgettable holiday meal.

In all, a winter getaway to London is both an adventure and a feast for the senses. With its blend of tradition, festive energy, and heartfelt warmth, London at Christmas is more than just a destination; it's an experience that lingers in memory, a chance to embrace the season with all its wonder and charm.

CHAPTER 2

ICONIC CHRISTMAS LIGHTS AND DISPLAYS

When it comes to Christmas lights and displays, London is a city that truly knows how to sparkle. Each year, as December approaches, London's streets and landmarks undergo a magical transformation. Iconic locations—some known worldwide and others tucked away as hidden gems—become illuminated with thousands of dazzling lights, creating scenes that are both breathtaking and memorable. The city's holiday lights are more than decorations; they're a celebration of winter and togetherness, designed to bring joy to everyone who experiences them.

London's Christmas light displays offer an enchanting way to explore the city. From the vibrant shopping hubs of

Oxford Street and Regent Street to the cozy charm of Covent Garden, each district brings its own unique flair to the season. Walking through these illuminated streets feels like stepping into a winter wonderland, each display capturing a different facet of the holiday spirit. Some displays reflect tradition, using warm, twinkling lights and classic festive colors. Others embrace modernity, featuring bold patterns, innovative designs, and even interactive installations that let you become part of the scene. The lights are stunningly diverse, ensuring that each area feels distinct, yet all are connected by a shared sense of festive magic.

One of the most delightful aspects of London's holiday lights is the blend of the expected and the unexpected. Year after year, locals and visitors alike anticipate the lighting ceremonies on Oxford Street and Regent Street. These are grand, memorable events, where crowds gather to watch the switch-on, often accompanied by live performances and appearances by special guests. There's a sense of shared wonder as the lights come on, marking the official start of the Christmas season in the city.

But London's festive lights go beyond these famous streets. Covent Garden, with its giant Christmas tree and fairy-lit market stalls, brings an inviting, almost old-world charm that feels cozy and heartwarming. Meanwhile, Carnaby Street often surprises with themed displays that stand out from the traditional red and green. From colorful installations inspired by rock and roll to quirky, fun designs, Carnaby offers a creative twist that adds a playful energy to the season. This mix of the familiar and the unique is what makes exploring London's Christmas lights so exciting; no two areas feel quite the same, and each offers its own perspective on the holiday season.

Experiencing London's Christmas lights isn't just about seeing—it's about feeling the full sensory magic of the season. The streets are alive with the sounds of carols, the laughter of families, and the chatter of friends meeting to take in the lights together. Many areas, like Leicester

Square and Southbank, host festive markets alongside their displays, adding the comforting scents of mulled wine, spiced treats, and freshly roasted chestnuts to the air. The lights glimmer against the winter sky, reflecting off shop windows and even the occasional puddle, casting a glow that wraps the city in warmth.

Even the bustling crowds become part of the experience, with each passerby bundled up in coats and scarves, sharing in the sense of wonder. London's festive lights are more than just decorations—they're an invitation to pause, take a breath, and simply enjoy the beauty of the season. Whether you're marveling at the lights for the first time or returning as part of an annual tradition, the experience feels both familiar and endlessly enchanting.

In this chapter, we'll explore the details of London's most iconic light displays, from their history and the inspiration behind them to insider tips on when and where to experience them at their best. By the end, you'll have a roadmap for discovering the city's illuminated treasures, ready to experience the holiday magic that only a London Christmas can bring.

2.1 THE MOST STUNNING LIGHT DISPLAYS AROUND THE CITY

London's holiday season is famously marked by its dazzling light displays, which transform some of the city's busiest streets and squares into awe-inspiring winter wonderlands. Each display is uniquely designed, with its own personality and style, creating magical settings that seem straight out of a storybook.

At the top of any visitor's list should be Oxford Street. Year after year, Oxford Street pulls out all the stops, dressing its long avenue with hundreds of thousands of lights. The display here is grand and impressive, with rows of suspended lights casting a soft, enchanting glow on the bustling crowds below. Typically, the lights are turned on in early November with an extravagant ceremony that often includes live performances and celebrity guests. The best time to visit Oxford Street is in the early evening, just as the shops start closing and the lights take center stage, bathing the street in a tranquil, festive atmosphere.

Regent Street, just around the corner, offers an equally unforgettable sight. Known for its "Spirit of Christmas" display, Regent Street's lights feature elegant, larger-than-life angels that soar above the road. Their golden wings and gentle glow bring a sense of wonder that feels almost heavenly, making it one of the most photographed Christmas displays in London. Visiting Regent Street in the evening allows you to fully appreciate the warm, golden light and marvel at the intricate details in each wing. For those looking to avoid crowds, visiting during the weekday can provide a more peaceful experience without sacrificing any of the magic.

Covent Garden's holiday decorations add a distinctively cozy, old-world charm to the area.

This historic market square is adorned with thousands of fairy lights, a giant Christmas tree, and a beautifully decorated reindeer sculpture, creating an inviting, festive atmosphere. The display here feels traditional and intimate, as if stepping into a classic Christmas film. Covent Garden also offers a lively holiday market with food and drink stalls, making it the perfect place to sip on mulled wine or hot chocolate while enjoying the lights. Try visiting in the late afternoon to catch the tree as it lights up against the fading daylight, making for a stunning photo opportunity.

Each of these popular spots brings something special to London's holiday season. Together, they form a must-see lineup that showcases the city's unique flair for holiday decor, making it easy to understand why people travel from all over to witness them.

2.2 HIDDEN GEMS: OFF-THE-BEATEN-PATH LIGHT SHOWS

While London's main Christmas light displays are breathtaking, there are also lesser-known spots that offer a more intimate and equally enchanting experience. These hidden gems allow visitors to enjoy beautiful displays away from the crowds and often highlight the charm of local neighborhoods that tourists might otherwise overlook.

One such gem is Kew Gardens' Christmas at Kew, located in Richmond. The famous botanical gardens come alive each winter with a mesmerizing trail of lights that leads visitors through the grounds in a one-of-a-kind experience. The gardens are transformed with illuminated tunnels, laser projections on ancient trees, and breathtaking light installations that showcase nature's beauty in a whole new light. The magical atmosphere at Kew feels deeply personal and quiet, perfect for those looking for a more tranquil experience. Since tickets are limited, it's best to book in advance, and going on a weekday evening can provide a more serene visit without the weekend crowds.

In East London, Canary Wharf offers a modern twist on Christmas lights. Known for its sleek skyscrapers, the area lights up with innovative, artful displays that play with color, light, and movement. The displays often incorporate interactive elements, allowing visitors to engage with the lights directly. The reflections off the glass buildings and surrounding water create a truly unique experience. Canary Wharf's displays have a distinctly urban feel, combining festive lights with modern art. This area is quieter than central London, making it a great spot for those who want a relaxed yet vibrant holiday outing.

Another hidden treasure is Marylebone Village, a charming neighborhood that celebrates Christmas with understated yet elegant lights. This quaint area embraces a minimalist style, opting for warm, subtle lights that add to its cozy, village-like feel.

The independent shops and cafes along Marylebone High Street join in the festive spirit, decorating their storefronts and creating a welcoming atmosphere that feels like stepping into a traditional English Christmas. Visiting in the early evening, you can enjoy a quiet stroll, browse the unique shops, and perhaps stop for a hot drink in one of the many cozy cafes.

Greenwich Market is another fantastic off-the-beaten-path location that combines Christmas lights with a local, authentic charm. The historic market square is adorned with twinkling lights that enhance its character without overwhelming it. During the holiday season, Greenwich hosts festive market stalls selling handmade crafts, vintage decorations, and delicious treats, making it a wonderful place to shop for unique holiday gifts. Visiting in the evening, you can enjoy a relaxed atmosphere with a warm community feel that stands in refreshing contrast to the busier spots in central London.

Exploring these hidden gems gives you a deeper, more personal experience of London's Christmas spirit. Each of these spots showcases the city's holiday lights in its own special way, from grand botanical trails to quaint village streets. They offer a reminder that sometimes, the most memorable moments of the season can be found in the quiet, beautifully illuminated corners of the city.

CHAPTER 3

FESTIVE MARKETS AND SHOPPING EXPERIENCES

When it comes to festive shopping and holiday markets, London offers an experience that's as magical as it is unforgettable. With twinkling lights, warm scents of mulled wine and roasted chestnuts, and charming stalls brimming with unique gifts, the city's Christmas markets create a seasonal atmosphere that feels both heartwarming and exciting. Wandering through these markets isn't just about finding the perfect gifts; it's about immersing yourself in the holiday spirit, discovering local artisans, and experiencing London's unique take on holiday traditions.

London's holiday shopping experiences cater to everyone, from those seeking artisan crafts and one-of-a-kind pieces to families looking for a festive day out. With each market bringing its own distinctive charm, the city turns holiday shopping into a celebration itself. These markets don't just offer products; they tell stories through handmade crafts, carefully curated gifts, and foods that evoke the flavors of the season. From vintage items and eco-friendly products to gourmet treats, each market offers a variety of goods that reflect the creativity and diversity of the city. And for travelers, this is a chance to take home something truly special—items that aren't just souvenirs but memories of a London Christmas.

One of the city's most famous festive shopping experiences is Winter Wonderland in Hyde Park. This iconic market goes beyond the traditional stalls, offering visitors a full-scale winter extravaganza. From Bavarian-style wooden chalets selling handcrafted gifts and festive decor to carnival rides and ice skating, Winter Wonderland creates a magical village that feels like a seasonal escape. Families can enjoy rides and games, while couples can browse the cozy stalls or warm up in one of the pop-up bars offering mulled wine and hot chocolate. Visiting Winter Wonderland at dusk or early evening is ideal, as the lights create a warm, enchanting glow, adding to the experience.

Covent Garden, too, becomes a holiday haven during the Christmas season. Famous for its towering Christmas tree, sparkling lights, and festive displays, Covent Garden's holiday market offers a blend of high-end shopping and artisan stalls. The area's cobbled streets are lined with charming boutiques and pop-up stalls, perfect for those looking to find a unique gift or indulge in some festive treats. While Winter Wonderland has a lively, bustling vibe, Covent Garden provides a more traditional, intimate atmosphere, perfect for slow, leisurely browsing. In the evenings, live performances and carolers often add a joyful soundtrack to your shopping experience, making it feel like a scene from a classic Christmas story.

Southbank Centre's Winter Market, along the Thames, is a highlight for those looking for a more relaxed, cultural take on festive shopping. Wooden huts line the riverside, offering an array of handcrafted items, from leather goods to handmade jewelry. The food here is a big attraction, with vendors serving up international treats like German bratwurst, Belgian waffles, and hot cider. Southbank's market has an international flair that celebrates the city's diversity and brings together flavors from across the world. As you stroll along the riverside, with the London skyline as a backdrop, it's easy to lose yourself in the festive magic. Visiting on a weekday can help you avoid crowds and enjoy the riverside lights in a more peaceful setting.

And, London's festive shopping scene extends well beyond its markets. Department stores like Harrods, Selfridges, and Liberty London transform into holiday wonderlands, with elaborate window displays and entire sections dedicated to Christmas gifts, decorations, and specialty foods. Visiting these stores during the holiday season is like stepping into a fairytale—each floor decorated with stunning lights, baubles, and garlands, creating an immersive holiday atmosphere. Harrods, in particular, is known for its luxurious displays and exclusive holiday items, making it a must-see destination even if you're only window-shopping.

Selfridges on Oxford Street goes above and beyond, often showcasing whimsical holiday displays that range from classic to quirky, appealing to both adults and children. Liberty London, with its beautiful Tudor-style building, offers a unique blend of high-end and handmade goods, featuring artisan-crafted ornaments, seasonal fragrances, and exclusive holiday collections. Walking through these stores during the holiday season isn't just about shopping;

it's about experiencing the joy and elegance that London brings to the festive season.

This chapter dives into the diverse holiday shopping experiences that make London such a special destination in December. From bustling markets filled with handcrafted gifts to beautifully decorated department stores, London's festive shopping scene captures the true magic of the season. Whether you're searching for the perfect gift, looking to sample seasonal foods, or simply wanting to soak in the holiday atmosphere, these markets and stores offer experiences that turn shopping into something extraordinary.

3.1 TOP CHRISTMAS MARKETS IN LONDON

London's Christmas markets are a cornerstone of the holiday season, creating bustling villages of stalls that charm visitors with twinkling lights, seasonal scents, and festive music. Each market has its unique flair, from the grand spectacle of Winter Wonderland in Hyde Park to the intimate charm of smaller community markets, and they offer a variety of goods and foods that capture the holiday spirit.

Winter Wonderland, Hyde Park

One of the largest and most iconic, Winter Wonderland in Hyde Park goes far beyond a typical Christmas market. This festive hub is more like a winter-themed amusement park, with everything from artisan market stalls to thrilling rides, an ice rink, and even a giant observation wheel. The food scene here is equally memorable, with dozens of vendors selling holiday treats like German bratwurst, churros with hot chocolate, and freshly baked pretzels. For something more indulgent, visitors can warm up in one of the cozy alpine-style huts with mulled wine or explore the Bavarian Village, a dedicated section with German-style food and beer halls. Winter Wonderland's mix of family-friendly activities and cozy spots to relax makes it ideal for all ages, and it's a must-visit for first-timers wanting the full London Christmas experience.

Southbank   Centre   Winter   Market

Set along the scenic Thames River, the Southbank Centre Winter Market offers a stunning riverside backdrop with wooden chalets offering both festive and global fare, making it a popular spot for food lovers and explorers alike. Unlike the grandeur of Winter Wonderland, Southbank's market exudes a more relaxed, intimate atmosphere, perfect for a leisurely stroll while sipping a hot cider or browsing handcrafted gifts. From jewelry and leather goods to ceramics, the market vendors showcase a mix of local and international craftsmanship, providing plenty of options for unique gifts. The market also hosts festive events and live performances, making it a fantastic spot to unwind and soak up some seasonal charm in the heart of the city.

Leicester Square Christmas Market

Nestled in the heart of London's West End, Leicester Square transforms into a festive haven during the holidays. This Christmas market features a selection of handcrafted gifts, seasonal foods, and charming decorations that make it a convenient stop for theatergoers or shoppers exploring central London. Leicester Square also hosts a traditional Santa's Grotto, making it a perfect family-friendly destination. After shopping, visitors can settle down in one of the cozy seating areas and enjoy treats like mince pies and mulled wine, all while taking in the vibrant surroundings. Smaller than some of the other markets, Leicester Square's festive setup brings a touch of Christmas magic to one of the city's busiest areas, giving it an intimate feel amid the urban energy.

Covent Garden

Covent Garden is a holiday experience all its own, with the market square transforming into a winter wonderland, complete with one of London's tallest Christmas trees, sparkling lights, and live performances.

The market's holiday decorations alone make it worth visiting, and its central location means visitors can easily explore the nearby boutique shops, galleries, and cafes as well. Here, shoppers can find a range of high-end gifts and artisanal products, from luxury candles and holiday ornaments to gourmet treats and handmade crafts. For a particularly magical moment, stop by in the evening when live performers and choirs fill the square with festive cheer.

3.2 UNIQUE CHRISTMAS SHOPPING DESTINATIONS

London's holiday shopping scene extends beyond traditional markets, with department stores, boutique shops, and temporary pop-ups each offering their own festive charm. These locations provide shoppers with exclusive gifts, luxurious decorations, and seasonal treats, each adding a unique twist to the classic Christmas shopping experience.

Harrods

No festive shopping trip to London would be complete without a stop at Harrods, the world-renowned luxury department store in Knightsbridge. During the holiday season, Harrods becomes a dazzling display of lights, ornaments, and themed decorations, transforming each floor into a feast for the senses. From high-end holiday collections to exclusive designer gifts, Harrods offers a shopping experience that's as indulgent as it is festive. The Christmas World section on the lower ground floor is a must-see, with everything from intricately designed ornaments to gourmet treats and holiday hampers. Harrods' unique mix of luxury items and seasonal exclusives makes it a prime destination for those seeking something truly special for their loved ones.

Liberty   **London**

Known for its iconic Tudor-style architecture and carefully curated collections, Liberty London on Regent Street is a true treasure trove for holiday shoppers. This beloved store takes pride in offering a mix of high-end and artisan goods, making it an ideal spot to find one-of-a-kind gifts that reflect the creativity and quality of London artisans.

During Christmas, Liberty's holiday department is filled with whimsical ornaments, hand-crafted decorations, and exclusive holiday products that make it a delight to browse. The store's warm, intimate atmosphere and beautifully themed displays make Liberty feel like a cozy escape from the bustling city outside, offering an experience that's as memorable as the gifts themselves.

Selfridges

Selfridges, located on Oxford Street, is a staple for London Christmas shopping, with vibrant holiday window displays and themed sections that capture the season's joy and wonder. From luxurious clothing and accessories to exclusive holiday items, Selfridges offers an extensive range of products across all categories. During the holiday season, their Christmas Shop showcases a collection of unique ornaments, holiday decor, and gift options that are sure to impress. Selfridges also hosts pop-up shops, where local artisans and designers showcase exclusive pieces perfect for thoughtful gift-giving.

Beyond the shopping, the store's festive atmosphere, complete with seasonal decorations and holiday playlists, adds an extra layer of magic to each visit.

Christmas by the River at London Bridge
For a mix of traditional market charm and boutique shopping, Christmas by the River at London Bridge is a standout choice. This seasonal market is set against the stunning backdrop of Tower Bridge and the Shard, creating a picturesque holiday shopping environment. With stalls offering unique gifts, gourmet foods, and artisanal

products, it's a great place to find items that reflect the local culture and creativity. After shopping, visitors can relax with a warm drink while enjoying views of the Thames, making it an unforgettable addition to any Christmas itinerary. This market's location, combined with its selection of high-quality goods, makes it an excellent destination for both locals and visitors.

Each of these shopping destinations, from the grand displays of Harrods to the cozy feel of Liberty and the scenic beauty of Christmas by the River, provides a unique way to experience London's festive spirit. Shopping here isn't just about finding the perfect gift; it's about immersing yourself in the city's holiday culture, exploring its neighborhoods, and taking part in the celebrations that make London one of the world's most enchanting destinations at Christmas.

CHAPTER 4

CHRISTMAS CUISINE: WHERE AND WHAT TO EAT

London's culinary scene is extraordinary year-round, but at Christmas, it transforms into something truly magical. The holiday season brings a blend of festive flavors, rich traditions, and creative twists on classic dishes that give every meal a distinctly warm and joyful feel. From the aroma of roasting chestnuts on street corners to elaborate seasonal menus at London's top restaurants, experiencing the city's Christmas cuisine is a must for any holiday visitor. This chapter will take you through the most enticing spots to dine and the iconic dishes you absolutely need to try, creating a culinary journey that's bound to fill you with holiday cheer and warmth.

London offers countless options for food lovers, from classic British holiday fare to international flavors brought to life with a festive touch. Whether you're seeking a cozy pub with a roaring fire or an elegant fine-dining experience, the city has something for everyone. And, of course, there's always the added charm of beautifully decorated spaces, with twinkling lights, wreaths, and the unmistakable holiday ambiance that fills each venue.

One of the true joys of celebrating Christmas in London is indulging in traditional British holiday dishes that have been enjoyed for generations. These meals are steeped in history and rich in flavor, embodying the essence of the season.

Roast   Turkey   with   All   the   Trimmings
No Christmas meal in London would be complete without the traditional roast turkey. This classic dish is often served with all the comforting sides: roasted potatoes, parsnips, Brussels sprouts, and stuffing, typically accompanied by gravy and cranberry sauce. Many restaurants across London offer their own take on this beloved meal, from the grand dining rooms of hotels like The Savoy to charming pubs like The Churchill Arms in Kensington. You'll find a variety of settings where this holiday staple is served with elegance, adding a touch of British hospitality to your Christmas feast.

Christmas   Pudding   and   Mince   Pies
For dessert, you can't miss out on Christmas pudding and mince pies, two of Britain's most beloved holiday sweets. Christmas pudding, a rich, dense fruitcake doused in brandy and set aflame, is a delightful holiday tradition often served with brandy butter or custard. Meanwhile, mince pies—small, buttery pastry shells filled with a spiced mixture of dried fruits—are equally loved. Fortnum & Mason, an iconic London department store, offers some of the finest mince pies in the city, as well as a wide selection of beautifully packaged puddings perfect for gifts. These treats can also be found in abundance at holiday markets, where local bakers put their own spin on these classic desserts, making them an easy and delicious way to sample British holiday flavors on the go.

Pigs in Blankets

A playful but adored British side dish, pigs in blankets are bacon-wrapped sausages served alongside the main course in most Christmas dinners. This savory snack adds a flavorful, salty bite that contrasts beautifully with other rich holiday foods. Many gastropubs, such as The Wolseley in Piccadilly, serve pigs in blankets as part of their festive menus, letting you savor this comforting classic in a cozy, welcoming setting.

International Holiday Treats and Unique Food Experiences

London's diversity is perhaps best showcased through its food, and during the Christmas season, you'll find no shortage of international holiday treats that add global flavors to the festive spirit. Whether you're looking to try something new or want a taste of home, London's eclectic food scene has something special for you.

German Christmas Markets and Bratwurst
London's German-inspired Christmas markets, like those at Southbank Centre and Winter Wonderland, bring the warmth and charm of a traditional German Christmas to the city. These markets are famous for their bratwurst—juicy, flavorful sausages served in crusty rolls and topped with sauerkraut or mustard. Another popular treat here is the German potato pancake, or reibekuchen, often served with a dollop of sour cream or applesauce. These markets also offer glühwein, a hot mulled wine spiced with cinnamon, cloves, and citrus, which is perfect for warming up as you browse the holiday stalls.

Italian Panettone and Other Sweet Breads
Italian bakeries across London bring their own festive traditions to the holiday season with specialties like panettone, a sweet, airy bread studded with dried fruits. This delicacy has become increasingly popular in London, and during the holidays, many bakeries and department stores, including Harrods and Eataly, offer beautiful gift-

wrapped versions that make for an indulgent treat or a lovely present. You'll also find pandoro, a similar Italian bread without the fruits, often dusted with powdered sugar for a snowy effect.

These delicious breads are perfect for breakfast with a cup of coffee or as a dessert after a holiday meal.

French Pastries and Festive Bûche de Noël
The French influence on London's culinary landscape is unmistakable, especially during the holidays. Many French patisseries, such as PAUL and Ladurée, bring the festive bûche de Noël (or yule log) to their holiday menus. This decadent dessert is made from layers of sponge cake and creamy filling, often decorated with intricate chocolate designs that resemble a log. French bakeries also offer delicate pastries like éclairs, macarons, and tarts that make for perfect holiday indulgences or elegant gifts. Exploring these bakeries not only satisfies your sweet tooth but also adds a touch of European elegance to your Christmas experience.

In a city as diverse as London, every meal can be a festive adventure during the holiday season. Each dish, whether traditional or international, tells a story and captures the warmth and wonder of Christmas in its flavors and presentation. Dining here isn't just about food; it's about embracing the season, discovering new tastes, and sharing the joy of the holidays in one of the world's most enchanting cities.

4.1

TRADITIONAL CHRISTMAS DISHES IN LONDON

When it comes to holiday meals, few places do Christmas classics quite like London. Each dish tells a story of British tradition and brings with it the flavors of warmth, nostalgia, and celebration. The festive season in London presents the perfect chance to dive into these time-honored favorites and experience them where they're celebrated most authentically. From bustling markets to refined dining rooms, let's explore where you can find the best traditional British holiday dishes and what makes each one a cherished part of the season.

Mince Pies: A Taste of History
Mince pies are a quintessential part of a British Christmas. With a golden, flaky crust filled with sweet, spiced fruit, these little pies have been enjoyed for centuries, evolving from medieval recipes once filled with minced meat and spices. Now, they're a sweet delight infused with dried fruits, brandy, and a hint of cinnamon, often enjoyed with a cup of tea by the fire. Fortnum & Mason, a British institution, serves up some of the finest mince pies in the city, with their luxurious versions filled with quality ingredients and wrapped in charming holiday packaging. For a more traditional experience, Borough Market's artisan stalls also offer freshly baked mince pies that are simple, comforting, and made with love.

The Classic British Roast Dinner
Nothing says Christmas dinner in Britain like a classic roast. A roasted turkey or goose is typically served with

crispy roast potatoes, Brussels sprouts, buttery parsnips, and a rich gravy made from the meat's own juices. This dish feels like home on a plate, full of warm, hearty flavors that celebrate the best of winter produce. To experience an exceptional British roast, try The Savoy Grill, a Gordon Ramsay restaurant offering a lavish take on the Christmas roast, complete with all the trimmings in an elegant, historic setting. For a more rustic vibe, head to The Harwood Arms in Fulham, a beloved gastropub that crafts its festive roasts with the freshest local ingredients.

Mulled Wine: The Essence of Christmas in a Cup
One of the most delightful parts of exploring London at Christmas is warming up with a cup of mulled wine. This spiced, heated red wine is infused with cinnamon, cloves, and oranges, creating a cozy, festive aroma that fills the air at Christmas markets and pubs alike. Winter Wonderland in Hyde Park is a fantastic spot to grab a cup as you stroll through the vibrant stalls, or you can visit The Churchill Arms in Kensington, where you can enjoy mulled wine in one of London's most festively decorated pubs, surrounded by thousands of twinkling lights and holiday decorations.

4.2

DINING EXPERIENCES WORTH TRYING

London takes festive dining to the next level with immersive and themed holiday dining experiences that make every meal a memorable celebration. The city's restaurants and tearooms pull out all the stops, transforming into wonderlands of yuletide cheer, with menus tailored for the season. Whether you're indulging in a whimsical afternoon tea or a lavish holiday feast, these dining experiences are a true highlight of Christmas in London.

Themed   Holiday   Afternoon   Teas
Afternoon tea is a cherished British tradition, and at

Christmastime, it becomes something truly special. Many of London's finest hotels offer Christmas-themed afternoon teas, complete with holiday-inspired pastries, sandwiches, and spiced teas. At Claridge's, you can experience a luxurious holiday tea in a setting filled with opulent decorations, intricate gingerbread displays, and exquisite pastries crafted to reflect the flavors of the season.

For a more whimsical approach, try The Chesterfield Mayfair, where the Winter Wonderland afternoon tea includes snowman macarons, reindeer cupcakes, and warming mulled wine, creating a playful and enchanting treat for the senses.

Festive Menus at Iconic London Restaurants
For a full festive feast, some of London's most iconic restaurants roll out special Christmas menus that blend British tradition with creative flair. Sketch in Mayfair offers a holiday tasting menu that not only delights the palate but also immerses you in a world of art and design, with its eclectic décor and bold, artistic ambiance. Another notable spot is the Ivy Chelsea Garden, which transforms

into a winter paradise, adorned with seasonal foliage and fairy lights, offering a festive menu featuring delicacies like lobster and Champagne risotto, and a showstopping Christmas pudding with brandy sauce. Dining here feels like stepping into a holiday fairytale, with each dish crafted to elevate the season's spirit.

Each of these festive dining experiences offers a unique way to taste and celebrate the best of Christmas in London, turning every meal into a memory and showcasing the city's culinary creativity in all its holiday glory. Whether you're savoring a classic dish or discovering a new seasonal favorite, London's food scene at Christmas is as magical as the city itself.

CHAPTER 5

HOLIDAY SHOWS AND PERFORMANCES

When it comes to holiday entertainment, London offers an unrivaled array of shows and performances that bring the festive season to life. From classic tales brought to the stage with heartwarming nostalgia to high-energy, modern productions that put a new spin on holiday cheer, London's holiday performances are as diverse as they are captivating. There's something for everyone: family-friendly pantomimes, breathtaking ballet, enchanting Christmas carols, and even a few quirky seasonal comedies to add a sprinkle of humor to the mix. Attending a holiday performance in London isn't just about the show itself; it's about experiencing the magic, warmth, and artistry that make this city a cultural beacon during the most wonderful time of the year.

Imagine walking through the frosty streets of London as night falls, with holiday lights twinkling above, and theaters glowing with anticipation for the evening's performances. Crowds are filled with excitement, bundled in scarves and coats, as they head toward iconic venues like the Royal Albert Hall and the London Palladium. For many, attending these shows is a time-honored tradition, a way to connect with family and friends while being immersed in the season's festive spirit.

This chapter will guide you through some of the most unforgettable holiday shows and performances London has to offer. From timeless classics that have become holiday staples to hidden gems that locals cherish, we'll explore what makes each experience special and why they're worth adding to your festive itinerary.

Timeless Holiday Classics on Stage

If you're looking to experience the magic of Christmas through traditional tales and beloved stories, London has a lineup that will transport you into the heart of the season. The West End comes alive with spectacular productions that have become a cherished part of London's holiday celebrations.

From *The Nutcracker* ballet to *A Christmas Carol* , these performances are more than just shows—they're gateways into a world of wonder and nostalgia, where snowflakes dance and timeless characters come to life.

The   Nutcracker:
There's perhaps no show more synonymous with Christmas than *The Nutcracker* , Tchaikovsky's enchanting ballet that has captivated audiences for over a century. With its magical story of Clara and her journey to the Land of Sweets, accompanied by the iconic Dance of the Sugar Plum Fairy, *The Nutcracker* is a beautiful blend of festive storytelling and exquisite dance. The English National Ballet's performance at the London Coliseum is a breathtaking rendition, with lavish costumes, stunning set designs, and a score that captures the essence of holiday joy. Watching this ballet is an immersive experience—an

invitation to step into a winter wonderland where dreams come alive and Christmas spirit fills the air.

A Christmas Carol:
Charles Dickens' *A Christmas Carol* is another timeless holiday favorite that resonates deeply with audiences. The story of Ebenezer Scrooge's transformation from miser to kind-hearted gentleman captures the spirit of Christmas redemption, family, and goodwill. London's productions bring Dickens' Victorian London to life in a way that feels both nostalgic and relevant. The Old Vic's rendition is especially captivating, offering a unique, immersive staging that lets the audience feel like they're part of the story. The show combines haunting moments with joyful scenes, reminding everyone of the true meaning of Christmas. For fans of classic literature and heartwarming tales, *A Christmas Carol* is a must-see.

Unique Holiday Performances and Pantomimes

For those looking to experience something uniquely British and lighthearted, London's holiday season wouldn't be complete without the vibrant and humorous world of pantomime. These performances, filled with audience interaction, colorful costumes, and playful storytelling, are a favorite among locals and visitors alike. Combining fairy tales, slapstick comedy, and over-the-top theatrics, pantomimes bring laughter and cheer in a way that's completely distinct from traditional theater.

London's   Beloved   Pantomimes:
Pantomime is a holiday tradition unlike any other—a combination of comedy, music, and exaggerated performances that never fail to get the audience involved. From booing the villain to cheering on the hero, pantomime invites everyone to be part of the action. The London Palladium hosts some of the city's most popular pantomimes, with each year featuring a new story like *Cinderella* , *Aladdin* , or *Jack and the Beanstalk* . Star-studded casts and unexpected guest appearances make these shows an experience that's as exciting as it is

unpredictable. With bright costumes, catchy songs, and hilarious banter, pantomimes are perfect for families looking to enjoy a show that appeals to both children and adults.

Quirky   Seasonal   Performances:
For those wanting something a bit more offbeat, London has a selection of quirky holiday performances that offer a twist on the traditional. Venues like the Southbank Centre and smaller theaters across the city often stage unique productions that reinterpret holiday classics or introduce entirely original holiday tales. From dark comedies to musical parodies, these shows add a refreshing flavor to the season's entertainment lineup.

For example, *A Christmas Gaiety* at the Royal Albert Hall blends holiday joy with a lively celebration of LGBTQ+ culture, combining traditional carols with a modern twist. These performances provide an alternative way to celebrate the season, bringing humor, diversity, and creativity to the heart of London's festive offerings.

London's holiday shows and performances are a testament to the city's vibrant cultural scene, offering something for every type of theatergoer. Whether you're swept away by the grace of ballet, captivated by a Dickensian tale, or laughing along at a pantomime, these experiences capture the heart and soul of Christmas in London. The magic of seeing these performances is that they invite everyone—from seasoned theater fans to first-time viewers—to step into a world of festive delight, where tradition and creativity come together to make memories that last a lifetime.

5.1 MUST-SEE CHRISTMAS SHOWS AND PANTOMIMES

London's holiday theater scene is one of the highlights of the festive season, offering a blend of classic productions and whimsical pantomimes that have become a cherished part of the city's Christmas celebrations. Whether you're looking to immerse yourself in timeless tales or enjoy a fun-filled, interactive experience, London's theaters have something special for everyone.

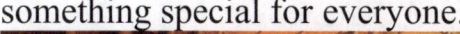

Christmas **A Carol:**

One of the most iconic holiday plays in London is *A Christmas Carol* , Charles Dickens' famous story of Ebenezer Scrooge's transformation from a miser to a man of compassion. The moral lessons of generosity, love, and redemption make this production a perfect fit for the holiday season. With its roots in Victorian England, *A Christmas Carol* brings the festive atmosphere of London's past to life. The story is often performed with a mix of traditional and modern adaptations, which brings a fresh twist to the beloved classic. The Old Vic's production, with its immersive set designs and moving performances, is a standout. The production often features a dynamic cast, creating a truly magical atmosphere, and offers an excellent opportunity to experience the essence of Christmas through theater.

Festive Pantomimes:

No Christmas in London is complete without a trip to one of the city's lively and colorful pantomimes. A staple of British holiday tradition, pantomimes are fun-filled performances that combine fairy tales, slapstick humor, catchy songs, and audience participation. They are designed to entertain the whole family, making them a perfect holiday outing for people of all ages.

Pantomimes often take familiar stories such as *Cinderella* , *Jack and the Beanstalk* , and *Aladdin* , and inject them with a modern, comedic twist. Expect to see larger-than-life characters, dazzling costumes, and plenty of playful banter between the performers and the audience. The London Palladium hosts one of the most famous pantomimes each year, drawing large crowds eager to enjoy the spectacle. The performances are always packed with energy, laughter, and surprises, with celebrity guest appearances adding to the excitement. If you're in the mood for something lighthearted and full of festive fun, a pantomime is a must-see experience.

These theater experiences bring a sense of joy and wonder that perfectly complements the holiday spirit. The holiday season wouldn't be complete without taking in one of London's famous Christmas performances, and whether you're captivated by the haunting beauty of *A Christmas*

Carol or caught up in the hilarious antics of a pantomime, you're bound to leave the theater with a smile on your face and the warmth of Christmas in your heart.

5.2 MUSICAL EVENTS AND CAROL CONCERTS

As much as London's theater scene lights up during the holidays, so does its rich tradition of music and carol concerts. London's musical performances and carol services are an integral part of the festive spirit, providing the city with an atmosphere of elegance, joy, and reflection. From grand concerts to intimate services, these performances offer a special way to celebrate the season and experience the heartwarming power of music.

Carol Services and Concerts: London is home to some of the world's most renowned choirs and musical venues, making it a prime destination for those seeking a truly festive experience through song. Iconic locations such as Westminster Abbey, St. Paul's Cathedral, and the Royal Albert Hall host some of the most anticipated carol concerts and services during Christmas. The carol services at Westminster Abbey are particularly famous, with the majestic architecture and ethereal acoustics providing the perfect backdrop for the choir's performance. Expect to hear beloved carols like *O Holy Night* , *Silent Night* , and *Hark! The Herald Angels Sing* , beautifully sung by choirs that have honed their craft throughout the year.

The Royal Albert Hall also hosts a series of Christmas concerts, including its famous *Christmas Carols by Candlelight* performance. With its grandiose atmosphere and sweeping ceilings, the venue is the perfect setting to enjoy a night of holiday music. These concerts typically feature a mix of traditional carols and classical music, accompanied by orchestras that evoke the true spirit of Christmas. Many concerts also include performances by soloists and instrumental ensembles, ensuring that each piece is delivered with a sense of grace and festive cheer.

Performances   by   Renowned   Choirs:
If you want to experience the beauty of London's choral music scene, the choirs of St. Paul's Cathedral and the BBC Singers are must-see attractions during the Christmas season. St. Paul's offers a stunning Christmas Eve service, which is a candlelit event featuring a choir that fills the majestic cathedral with angelic harmonies. The service is filled with warmth, peace, and a sense of tradition that is perfect for reflecting on the season's meaning.

The BBC Singers, on the other hand, are known for their beautiful renditions of Christmas music, from classical pieces to modern holiday arrangements. Their concerts, held at various venues in the city, offer a more intimate experience while still providing the rich, evocative sound that the BBC Singers are known for. Many concerts feature a mix of holiday music and contemporary pieces, blending the past and present to create an engaging and uplifting experience.

 For those
who love music, London's Christmas carol services and
concerts offer an unforgettable experience. Whether you're
sitting in a grand cathedral, listening to a choir's angelic
voices, or enjoying an orchestral concert at the Royal
Albert Hall, the city's musical offerings add an extra layer
of magic to the holiday season. The uplifting power of
carols and Christmas hymns fills the air with festive spirit
and a sense of connection to something larger than
ourselves—whether it's the beautiful music, the traditions
it celebrates, or the people around us.

From the heartwarming storytelling of *A Christmas Carol* to the timeless joy of carol concerts, London's holiday performances provide an essential experience for anyone visiting during the festive season. The theater and music scenes come together to create a vibrant tapestry of holiday cheer, making the city an unforgettable place to celebrate Christmas. Whether you're in the mood for a classic theater show or a soul-stirring concert, London offers an array of performances that will make your Christmas season truly special.

CHAPTER 6

FAMILY-FRIENDLY FESTIVITIES

Christmas in London isn't just for adults—it's a magical time for families to come together and make lasting memories. The city transforms into a wonderland of festive events, activities, and experiences that cater to all ages, from young children to teens and even the young at heart. The charm of London during the holiday season lies not only in its dazzling lights and grand displays but also in the abundance of family-friendly activities that are sure to delight and entertain. Whether you're looking to enjoy a cozy day out, explore interactive experiences, or witness awe-inspiring festive spectacles, London has something to offer every family.

The beauty of the holiday season in London is how it blends tradition with innovation, offering both timeless Christmas experiences and exciting new events that kids will love. From enchanting light displays to ice skating rinks, Santa's grottos to festive workshops, London's Christmas offerings are designed to create a festive spirit that children and parents alike can enjoy together. What sets this chapter apart is its ability to connect families with activities that engage their imagination, offer opportunities to bond, and deliver pure, unfiltered holiday joy.

In this chapter, we'll delve into the best of family-friendly festivities in London—activities that are fun, accessible, and filled with Christmas cheer. Whether you want to take a magical ride on a vintage carousel, marvel at life-sized gingerbread houses, or attend one of the spectacular holiday-themed events that make London feel like a scene from a Christmas movie, this guide will show you exactly where to go and what to do. Ready to create cherished memories with your loved ones this Christmas? Then let's discover the enchanting world of family-friendly festivities in London, where the spirit of the season comes alive in the most delightful ways.

6.1 TOP ATTRACTIONS FOR A KID-FRIENDLY CHRISTMAS

London is a city that knows how to make Christmas special for everyone, and when it comes to children, the festive season is full of magical attractions and experiences. The city's Christmas charm extends beyond the twinkling lights and festive displays, offering a wide variety of kid-friendly events and places to visit. Whether your little ones believe in the magic of Santa or simply love the festive fun of the season, these top attractions are sure to create memories that will last a lifetime.

 One of the most beloved traditions is visiting **Santa's Grotto** , where children can meet Father Christmas himself. The Grotto experiences around London are carefully curated to bring the story of Santa and his elves to life in the most

magical way. The grottos at locations like **Hamleys Toy Store** and **Kew Gardens** offer immersive, themed settings that transport kids into a world of wonder, where they can share their Christmas wishes with Santa and receive a small gift in return. These grottos are more than just a meet-and-greet; they are interactive, with festive characters and enchanting decorations that make the visit feel like a fairytale come true.

Another must-visit attraction is **Winter Wonderland** in Hyde Park. This large-scale event transforms the park into a Christmas dreamland, with an ice rink, carnival rides, games, circus shows, and themed attractions for kids of all ages.

The famous **Magical Ice Kingdom** is especially captivating for children, with life-sized ice sculptures and a snowy wonderland that will leave them in awe. For a more adventurous experience, children can try out the ice skating rink or go on thrilling rides like the giant Ferris wheel. It's an experience that captures the heart of Christmas magic, and parents will appreciate the festive atmosphere and family-friendly activities scattered throughout the park.

If you're looking for something more unique, consider visiting **Christmas at the Zoo** at **ZSL London Zoo** , where animals join in the holiday spirit with special Christmas-themed activities and decorations. Children will be entertained while learning about the zoo's animals, and they'll love the chance to see them interact with festive treats or holiday-themed enclosures.

These attractions not only capture the festive magic of London but are also designed to keep kids engaged and excited throughout the holiday season. With so many options to explore, London offers something for every family, making it an unforgettable destination for a kid-friendly Christmas adventure.

6.2 HANDS-ON EXPERIENCES FOR KIDS

For families looking for a more interactive and creative way to celebrate the holidays, London offers a fantastic range of **hands-on experiences** that will spark a child's imagination and creativity. These activities allow kids to get involved in crafting, cooking, and learning through play—transforming the traditional Christmas celebration into an educational and hands-on adventure.

One of the most popular types of activities is **Christmas workshops** . Many art studios and galleries in London host workshops where children can make their own Christmas crafts, from festive cards and decorations to gingerbread houses and personalized gifts. At places like the **V&A**

Museum of Childhood or the **Natural History Museum** , kids can participate in special holiday-themed sessions where they can explore their artistic talents and take home something unique to commemorate the day. These workshops allow children to embrace the spirit of giving by creating personalized crafts for their family or friends, all while having fun in a guided, creative environment.

For those who prefer to get their hands dirty in the kitchen, **baking classes** are a fun way to learn holiday recipes. Many bakeries and food venues in London offer Christmas-themed baking experiences, where children can decorate their own cookies, cupcakes, or even try their hand at creating a traditional Christmas pudding. **Biscuiteers** and **Borough Market** are popular locations that host child-friendly baking events where families can bond over flour and frosting while learning how to make festive treats. These classes are perfect for kids who enjoy the sweet side of Christmas and offer an interactive way to make holiday memories that can be enjoyed at home.

In addition to crafting and cooking, kids can also take part in **holiday storytelling sessions** . Several venues around London, such as the **Southbank Centre** , host festive storytelling sessions where children can listen to traditional Christmas tales or even get involved in creating their own holiday stories. These sessions often include interactive elements, like acting out parts of the story or creating props and costumes, which keeps children entertained while allowing them to unleash their creativity and imagination.

Interactive Christmas experiences are a fantastic way for children to feel involved in the holiday festivities, and London's vibrant arts and culture scene offers plenty of options. Whether they're making their own decorations, baking delicious treats, or engaging in a fun storytelling adventure, these hands-on experiences give children a chance to connect with the holiday season in meaningful ways.

 Not only do they provide an escape from the usual holiday shopping chaos, but they also foster a sense of creativity, joy, and community that kids will cherish long after Christmas is over.

CHAPTER 7

EXPLORING LONDON'S HISTORICAL CHRISTMAS TRADITIONS

Christmas in London isn't just about lights, shopping, and festive markets; it's a deep-rooted celebration that draws from centuries of traditions and customs, many of which have shaped the way we celebrate the holiday today. The city has a rich history of holiday rituals, events, and tales that make Christmas here a truly unique experience. From Dickensian charm to royal celebrations, London's Christmas traditions are a beautiful blend of the old and new, offering visitors a glimpse into the city's past while enjoying its present-day festive vibrancy.

As you walk through London's streets during Christmas, you'll be tracing footsteps that go back hundreds of years—where horse-drawn carriages once delivered gifts, where Christmas markets were first established, and where grand feasts were held for the wealthy, while the poor gathered in churchyards for solace and song. The city's rich history gives every corner a story, and exploring London's Christmas traditions allows you to experience the holiday in a way that's deeply tied to the past.

In this chapter, we will take you on a journey through the historical Christmas traditions that have shaped the London we know today. From the Victorian-era celebrations inspired by Charles Dickens, to the regal Christmases of the British monarchy, to the long-standing customs that Londoners still uphold, you will uncover the fascinating stories and customs that make Christmas in the city unlike anywhere else in the world.

Prepare to immerse yourself in the rich tapestry of Christmas history that has made London a top destination for holiday travelers. These traditions are not only the heart of London's holiday spirit, but they also serve as a reminder of the timeless joy that Christmas brings, generation after generation. So, let's step back in time and explore the historical traditions that continue to make Christmas in London an unforgettable experience.

7.1 A LOOK AT LONDON'S FESTIVE PAST

London's history is intertwined with centuries of holiday traditions that have evolved, but at their heart, the Christmas season has always been about family, community, and celebration. To understand Christmas in London today, one must first look at its fascinating festive past, where Victorian-era influences, ancient rituals, and royal customs all came together to shape the holiday we know and love.

In the 19th century, London underwent a transformation during the reign of Queen Victoria. The Victorian period marked the rise of many of the Christmas traditions we cherish today. It was a time when Christmas became a family-oriented holiday rather than a more formal, church-centered observance. Charles Dickens played a pivotal role in popularizing Christmas as a time for charitable giving, family gatherings, and goodwill to all. His famous novella

A Christmas Carol (1843) captured the spirit of the time, with its portrayal of Scrooge's redemption and the importance of generosity and family.

CHRISTMAS IN LONDON
1705.

QUEEN ANNE.

Victorian Christmases were lavish affairs for the wealthy, with grand feasts, decorated homes, and public celebrations. The tradition of decorating Christmas trees, inspired by Queen Victoria and Prince Albert's adoption of the German custom, became a staple in London households. The first Christmas tree in London's royal family was displayed at Windsor Castle in 1841, and soon after, the trend caught on throughout the city. Streets like Oxford Street were festooned with lights and garlands, and Christmas markets became common sights where Londoners could shop for seasonal treats, handmade goods, and gifts.

Yet, while the wealthy celebrated in grand style, Christmas was also a time for those less fortunate. Public charity events flourished, and the poor often found solace in church services and communal Christmas dinners. The sense of community and inclusivity has remained a defining aspect of London's festive season, with events that encourage giving and charity still a central part of the celebrations today.

Fast forward to the present day, and while much has changed, the legacy of Victorian Christmas traditions continues to shape how London celebrates the season. The city's festive past is still evident in its markets, its lights, and its love for community-driven events. Visiting London during Christmas is like stepping back in time, with the city's historic charm still evident in every corner, from its grand department stores to its historic pubs. In many ways, London's Christmas traditions have become a blend of old and new—keeping the best of the past while embracing modern celebrations and festivities.

CELEBRATING IN HISTORIC LOCATIONS

There's no better way to experience the festive season in London than by celebrating in one of the city's historic venues, where the past and present seamlessly blend. These iconic locations don't just offer a glimpse into history—they provide an atmosphere rich with seasonal magic, making Christmas in these historic sites an unforgettable experience.

One of the most remarkable places to celebrate Christmas is **Hampton Court Palace** , a former royal residence of Henry VIII, whose grand banquets and seasonal feasts have long been part of British Christmas traditions. Today, visitors can experience a truly regal Christmas at Hampton Court, where the Palace is transformed into a winter wonderland. The historic kitchens are decked out to showcase how Christmas feasts would have been prepared during the Tudor era, and visitors can take part in candlelit tours, discover centuries-old holiday recipes, and even enjoy a Christmas carol service in the grand Chapel. Walking through the palace's splendid rooms, you'll feel as though you've stepped back into a festive court from a bygone era.

Another historic venue that makes for a spectacular Christmas destination is **the Tower of London** . Dating back to 1066, the Tower is not only a fortress and royal palace but also a place of tradition and intrigue. During the Christmas season, the Tower hosts special events that delve into the history of Christmas in medieval England. Explore the grand halls, where you can learn about royal Christmas customs from centuries ago, and discover how the monarchs of the past celebrated the season. The Tower also hosts various festive workshops, including storytelling sessions for children, where they can learn about the Tower's rich history through the lens of Christmas folklore and tales.

For a truly magical Christmas experience, the **Royal Albert Hall** offers a historic venue for musical performances that have been celebrated for decades. Its traditional Christmas concerts, including the annual *Royal Choral Society Christmas Concert* , provide a chance to hear carols performed by some of the world's finest choirs in a magnificent, historic setting. The hall's architecture, combined with the powerful sound of carolers echoing through the grand space, creates an atmosphere of pure festive magic.

These venues are more than just locations—they are the living, breathing embodiment of London's history and culture. Each one holds stories of royal celebrations, medieval feasts, and centuries of tradition that continue to be passed down through the generations. Visiting these historic locations during Christmas is like witnessing the past come alive. The grand settings, the period decorations, and the festive activities all combine to make for an immersive experience that will transport you to a

Christmas long ago, while still offering the joy and spirit of the holiday that makes London's Christmas so special today.

For those seeking a true sense of London's festive past, these historic venues offer an unparalleled experience that combines history, tradition, and the magic of the season. Whether it's the royal palaces, ancient castles, or the grand concert halls, celebrating Christmas in these iconic locations is an opportunity to connect with the rich heritage of London, making this holiday season one to remember.

CHAPTER 8

LONDON'S WINTER OUTDOOR ACTIVITIES

When the winter chill settles over London, the city transforms into a wonderland of festive energy, brimming with outdoor activities that make the most of the season's crisp air and festive spirit. London's winter charm is undeniable, and there is no shortage of ways to embrace the cold while enjoying all that the city has to offer. Whether you're looking to explore the great outdoors, engage in seasonal sports, or simply soak up the beauty of London's winter landscapes, the city offers a wide range of activities to create unforgettable winter memories.

Winter in London is a special time when outdoor spaces come alive with both traditional activities and unique experiences. As the weather grows colder, many of London's outdoor parks, squares, and historical sites take on a magical glow. The city offers a perfect balance of excitement and relaxation, where you can take in breathtaking views of winter landscapes, glide on ice at world-famous rinks, or simply wander through festive markets and enjoy the lights and sounds of the season.

In this chapter, we'll explore some of the most exciting outdoor activities that London has to offer during the winter months. From outdoor ice skating rinks, with their twinkling lights and festive atmosphere, to scenic walks along the Thames, London invites visitors to experience the joy of winter through its outdoor experiences. For those who want to dive into the heart of the holiday season, there are countless activities that combine sport, culture, and the city's historical charm, making it an ideal destination for those seeking adventure in the winter months.

As we dive into the winter activities London has to offer, you'll see that this season is not just about staying indoors by the fire. It's about embracing the chill and enjoying the city's vibrant outdoor culture—an experience that will leave you with lasting memories and a deeper appreciation for all that London has to offer during the wintertime. Whether you're traveling with family, friends, or as a solo adventurer, London's winter outdoor activities ensure there's something for everyone, making it a top winter destination for locals and visitors alike.

8.1 ICE SKATING AND WINTER SPORTS

When winter settles over London, one of the most beloved and exhilarating activities that comes to life is ice skating. There's something undeniably magical about gliding across a glittering ice rink under the twinkling lights of the season. Whether you're a seasoned skater or a first-timer, London's outdoor ice rinks provide the perfect blend of festive spirit and sporting fun, making them an essential part of the city's winter charm.

One of the most iconic ice skating venues in London is **Somerset House** . Nestled in the heart of the city, this historic courtyard transforms into a winter wonderland each year. The rink is surrounded by majestic stone columns and elegant 18th-century architecture, creating a spectacular backdrop for skating. The rink itself is large, offering plenty of space for both beginners and experienced skaters. For those who want to take their experience to the next level, Somerset House also hosts DJ nights, themed skating sessions, and a pop-up skate shop, all adding to the atmosphere of festivity. The rink at Somerset House is open from November through January, and booking in advance is highly recommended due to its popularity during the holiday season.

Another top ice skating destination is **Canary Wharf** , which offers a sleek, modern setting for ice skating. This rink is one of the largest in the city, providing a spacious area for skaters to glide under the canopy of lights. The surrounding business district adds a cosmopolitan flair to the experience, while the rink itself is known for its smooth ice and wintery ambiance. After skating, you can warm up with mulled wine or hot chocolate from the rink-side café, enjoying the views of the nearby skyscrapers as they are lit up for the season. Canary Wharf is a favorite for those looking to combine skating with the excitement of a busy city atmosphere. This rink is typically open from mid-November to early January, and, like Somerset House, it can get crowded, so it's worth planning ahead.

For those seeking a more intimate, lesser-known skating experience, **Winter Wonderland in Hyde Park** offers a festive ice rink with a lively, fun atmosphere. In addition to the main rink, Winter Wonderland also features a range of other winter sports activities, including a funfair and themed games, making it a great destination for families or groups.

To truly enjoy these winter sports experiences, be sure to dress warmly in layers and waterproof gear to stay comfortable on the ice. Renting skates is often an option at most rinks, but if you plan to skate often, you might consider bringing your own for a better fit. Most rinks also offer skating aids for beginners, so if you're not confident on the ice, you can still have a blast with some extra support. Booking your tickets early is always a good idea, as these rinks can fill up quickly, especially during the peak holiday period.

8.2 WINTER WALKS AND PARKS

While ice skating provides an active winter experience, sometimes the best way to embrace London's winter charm is by taking a leisurely stroll through its many parks and scenic walks. When the city is covered in frost and the trees are bare, the beauty of London's green spaces takes on a new, serene appeal. Whether you're looking for a peaceful escape or simply want to explore the city's wintery side, these parks offer the perfect places to enjoy the season.

 **Hyde Park**
is one of London's largest and most famous parks, and in winter, it becomes a magical place to explore. Whether you're walking along the Serpentine, where you can often spot winter ducks and swans, or strolling through the tree-lined paths dusted with snow, Hyde Park offers tranquility in the midst of the bustling city. The park's grand expanse

means there's plenty of space to roam, and the crisp winter air makes the experience all the more refreshing. In addition to its natural beauty, Hyde Park is home to **Winter Wonderland** , where visitors can explore Christmas markets, enjoy the ice skating rink, or take a spin on the Ferris wheel. Even if you're not looking for amusement rides, just wandering around this iconic park during the winter months is an experience that captures the holiday spirit perfectly.

For a more secluded winter walk, **Richmond Park** is the place to go. Situated a little further out of central London, this expansive park offers sweeping views over deer-filled meadows and ancient woodlands. During the winter months, the park takes on a unique charm, with the bare trees and chilly air creating a peaceful, almost magical atmosphere. Richmond Park is famous for its free-roaming deer, which you can often spot grazing or wandering through the foggy mornings. It's an excellent location for a quiet walk to clear your head, or to take in the beauty of the winter landscape. The crisp winter air makes this park particularly refreshing for those looking to escape the noise of the city, and the long, winding paths are perfect for reflective strolls.

If you're looking for something closer to the city center, **St. James's Park** offers another winter gem. With its picturesque lake, and iconic views of Buckingham Palace, St. James's Park is a stunning location for winter walks.

The park's unique charm during the colder months comes from the contrast between its elegant tree-lined pathways and the serene, glassy surface of the lake. The park is a favorite for tourists, as well as locals, and it's a peaceful spot to take in London's winter beauty while being just steps away from some of the city's most famous landmarks.

When taking winter walks in these parks, it's always a good idea to wear comfortable shoes, as some of the paths can get slippery in cold weather. A warm hat and gloves will help you stay cozy, but be sure to dress in layers to adjust as you walk. Each park has its own unique winter appeal, from the grandeur of Hyde Park to the peaceful solitude of Richmond Park, and they're all perfect places to connect with nature and embrace the season.

These parks offer an inviting escape into winter's embrace, where you can experience the true beauty of London at its most serene and picturesque.

CHAPTER 9

SEASONAL TOURS AND UNIQUE SIGHTSEEING

As winter sweeps through London, the city takes on a different life—one that's filled with seasonal magic, festive cheer, and a charm that you simply can't experience at any other time of the year. The holiday season offers a unique opportunity to explore some of London's most iconic landmarks and hidden gems with a seasonal twist. Whether you're a visitor or a local looking to experience the city in a fresh way, seasonal tours and unique sightseeing experiences will provide you with unforgettable moments. From festive walking tours through twinkling streets to cozy river cruises, there's a whole new layer of London waiting to be discovered.

Winter months in London are packed with unique sightseeing opportunities, where historical landmarks and cultural spots are enhanced by holiday displays, glittering lights, and a festive atmosphere. **Seasonal tours** are an excellent way to uncover the hidden stories of the city. Many tours are designed specifically for the holiday season, bringing history and culture to life in new and exciting ways. These tours offer more than just a visit to the usual spots—they immerse you in a London that sparkles with the festive spirit, and they often feature lesser-known stories, fun facts, and experiences you won't get from a typical guidebook.

Imagine strolling through the streets of **Covent Garden** , where the air is filled with the scent of mulled wine and the sound of carolers, or hopping on a vintage double-decker bus for a **Christmas lights tour** that takes you past some of the most stunning holiday displays in the city. These seasonal tours give you the chance to explore the magic of London from a different perspective. Each stop on these tours is carefully chosen to highlight the holiday spirit while showcasing the city's rich history, from festive decorations on historic buildings to the time-honored traditions that have been passed down through generations.

For those who want to see London from a unique angle, seasonal **sightseeing tours** also include options like **Christmas river cruises** along the Thames, which offer incredible views of the city's iconic landmarks illuminated for the season. Imagine sipping hot chocolate as you float past the Tower of London, the London Eye, and St. Paul's Cathedral—all beautifully adorned for the holidays. These cruises offer a cozy, festive way to enjoy London's sights while avoiding the winter chill on land.

 London's rich tapestry of history and culture means that sightseeing is not limited to the major attractions alone. With so much to see and experience, the winter season adds a layer of magic to every corner of the city, making it the perfect time to embark on a seasonal tour or sightseeing adventure. Whether you're looking for a festive twist on a traditional London tour or a completely unique experience, this chapter will guide you through the most enchanting and exclusive ways to explore London during the holiday season. Let's delve into the best seasonal tours and the unique sightseeing experiences that will make your visit to London unforgettable this winter.

9.1 CHRISTMAS-THEMED CITY TOURS

London transforms during the Christmas season, and one of the best ways to experience the city's festive spirit is through a **Christmas-themed city tour** . These tours offer a unique opportunity to explore London's iconic landmarks and charming neighborhoods, all while enjoying the sparkling lights, decorations, and the overall holiday atmosphere. From hopping on a **festive bus ride** to taking a **charming walking tour** , these experiences bring a new dimension to sightseeing in London, especially when the city is at its most magical.

One of the most popular options is a **Christmas lights bus tour** , where you can ride in comfort through some of the best-lit streets in the city. This includes iconic areas such as **Oxford Street** , **Regent Street** , and **Covent Garden** , all adorned with thousands of sparkling lights. These bus tours often come with a knowledgeable guide who shares fascinating stories behind the displays and explains the history of London's Christmas traditions. As you sit back and enjoy the warmth of the bus, you'll be able to see the city from a completely different perspective. The sight of

London's grand streets illuminated in festive splendor is a memory you won't soon forget.

For those who prefer to be more active, **walking tours** provide a fantastic way to experience London up close and personal. These tours often focus on areas like **Hyde Park** and **Leadenhall Market**, where Christmas markets, pop-up shops, and cozy pubs line the streets. A guided walking tour through these areas can give you insider tips about the best places to shop for gifts, enjoy a seasonal treat, or simply take in the sights. Many walking tours also incorporate London's rich history, so you'll get a blend of festive cheer and fascinating historical insights along the way.

If you want to see the city from a different angle, a **Christmas river cruise** along the Thames is a must. Gliding past landmarks such as **the Tower of London**, **Big Ben**, and **St. Paul's Cathedral**, all dressed up for the season, offers breathtaking views that you won't get from the streets. These cruises typically include hot drinks, seasonal snacks, and a guide to highlight the city's landmarks as you pass them. The relaxed pace of the river cruise provides an intimate and picturesque experience, ideal for couples or families looking to unwind while taking in the beauty of the city's holiday lights.

9.2 HIDDEN CHRISTMAS SPOTS AND SECRET VIEWPOINTS

While London's major holiday spots like Oxford Street and Covent Garden are a must-see, there's something truly special about discovering the **hidden Christmas spots** and **secret viewpoints** that are off the typical tourist radar. These lesser-known locations allow you to experience the quieter, more peaceful side of Christmas in London, and they often come with fewer crowds, making them perfect for those who prefer a more intimate holiday experience.

One of these hidden gems is **Neal's Yard** , a vibrant, tucked-away courtyard in **Covent Garden** . While it's a popular spot year-round, it becomes even more magical during the Christmas season. The small square is decorated with twinkling fairy lights, and the atmosphere is cozy and charming. It's a great place to grab a hot drink from one of the nearby cafes, wander around the colorful alleys, and soak in the festive spirit without the hustle and bustle of the bigger crowds.

Another secret viewpoint can be found at **Primrose Hill** , a scenic hilltop park located just north of Regent's Park. From the top of the hill, you'll get a sweeping view of London's skyline, which looks even more spectacular when illuminated by the Christmas lights of the city. This spot offers a peaceful and serene experience, and it's especially beautiful at sunset when the city's glow starts to take over the horizon.

For a truly unique experience, visit **Hampstead Heath** —a large, green space on the outskirts of central London. The heath offers panoramic views of the city, and during winter, it's an ideal place to take a walk while enjoying the fresh, crisp air. The **Parliament Hill** viewpoint on Hampstead Heath provides one of the best views of London's skyline, particularly stunning at dusk when the city is bathed in the warm, golden light of the holiday season.

If you're looking for a quieter and more intimate view of Christmas in London, consider exploring the **South Bank** at night. While the area around the London Eye can be busy, if you walk a little farther along the river, you'll discover peaceful spots where you can sit by the water, enjoy the twinkling lights of the **Southbank Centre** , and watch the boats drift by. It's the perfect place for a quiet moment with a view of London dressed up for the holidays.

For those who want to mix a bit of Christmas cheer with London's hidden gems, there's **Kensington Gardens** . While the gardens are lovely year-round, in winter, the area around **Kensington Palace** looks particularly beautiful, with the palace grounds and surrounding trees decorated with twinkling lights. The more relaxed atmosphere of this area gives it a charming, almost fairytale-like quality that's perfect for a winter stroll.

Whether you're taking a guided Christmas tour through London's most famous streets or venturing off the beaten path to discover hidden gems and secret viewpoints, there's no shortage of ways to explore London's holiday magic. These seasonal tours and lesser-known spots allow you to enjoy the festive season in a way that feels personal, intimate, and unforgettable. So grab your winter coat, put on your walking shoes, and get ready to discover the best of London at Christmas, both the well-known and the secret sides of this spectacular city.

CHAPTER 10

HOLIDAY ACCOMMODATION: WHERE TO STAY

When planning a festive getaway to London, choosing the right place to stay is an essential part of creating an unforgettable holiday experience. The city offers a wide variety of accommodations, from luxurious hotels adorned with festive cheer to cozy boutique stays and unique holiday rentals that provide a home away from home. Whether you're looking for a glamorous stay in the heart of the city or a tranquil retreat on the outskirts, London has something to suit every style, preference, and budget. In this chapter, we will explore the best places to stay during the Christmas season, offering you a comprehensive guide to help make your stay as comfortable, enjoyable, and memorable as possible.

As London dresses itself in festive lights and decorations, the right accommodation can elevate your holiday experience. Imagine waking up to a snowy view of iconic landmarks, or stepping outside to be just a short stroll away from the Christmas markets, holiday shows, and all the seasonal magic the city has to offer. The right location, ambiance, and amenities can transform your visit into something special, making it easier for you to dive into the heart of London's festive atmosphere.

London's diverse neighborhoods offer a mix of traditional charm, modern luxury, and everything in between. From **luxury hotels with elaborate Christmas displays** to quaint **bed-and-breakfasts** in historical districts, and even charming **apartments in tucked-away corners of the city** , there's a perfect place for every traveler. Whether you prefer to stay near the vibrant **West End** , with its dazzling lights and shows, or in quieter, more intimate neighborhoods like **Notting Hill** or **Greenwich** , your accommodation will play an important role in shaping your London Christmas experience. In the pages that follow, we'll dive into different areas of London and explore the best holiday stays each one has to offer, ensuring that you find the ideal place to rest your head after a busy day of exploration and enjoyment.

BEST HOTELS FOR A FESTIVE STAY

For those who want to immerse themselves in the luxury and grandeur of London during the Christmas season, there is no shortage of high-end hotels that go all out with their festive décor, seasonal activities, and top-tier services. The best hotels for a festive stay not only offer exceptional comfort and prime locations, but they also transform into winter wonderlands, offering guests a truly magical experience.

At the **Claridge's Hotel** , located in Mayfair, Christmas is nothing short of spectacular. The hotel is renowned for its lavish holiday decorations, often created by world-renowned designers, and the grand lobby feels like stepping into a fairy tale. You can indulge in their **Christmas afternoon tea** , complete with seasonal treats, or enjoy an elegant **Christmas Day lunch** . Its central location means you're just a short walk from the **West End theatres** and **Oxford Street** , which are both illuminated in spectacular lights.

For a more modern and stylish Christmas experience, the **Shangri-La Hotel** in The Shard offers sweeping views of the city, as well as a festive atmosphere that reflects the cosmopolitan feel of London. With rooms offering panoramic views of the **London Eye** and **St. Paul's Cathedral** , it's the perfect place to stay if you want to enjoy London's sparkling skyline in a holiday setting. Their seasonal offerings often include special **cocktail menus** and **holiday spa treatments** , making it a luxury retreat.

If you're looking for something more traditional yet equally magical, **The Ritz London** in Piccadilly is a landmark in itself during Christmas. The Ritz becomes a stunning sight, with its grand tree and intricate decorations. Guests can experience the magic of the season with luxurious Christmas packages that include festive meals, cocktails, and even **Christmas Eve gala dinners** . Its prime location ensures you're in the heart of everything, with shopping districts and Christmas markets right at your doorstep.

For those seeking a more intimate and personal experience, **The Goring Hotel** in Belgravia offers a cozy, family-oriented atmosphere. This hotel is known for its service and personalized touches. During Christmas, the hotel features festive decorations that create a welcoming and homey ambiance, perfect for families looking to enjoy a peaceful holiday while still being close to the excitement of the city.

10.2 COZY ALTERNATIVES: B&BS, INNS, AND MORE

If you're seeking a more intimate, cozy, and affordable way to experience the holidays in London, there are plenty of **charming B&Bs, boutique hotels** , and **holiday rentals** that offer a unique and welcoming atmosphere. These alternative accommodations provide a quieter, more personalized experience, often situated in quieter corners of the city while still being within reach of the festive excitement.

One such place is **The Laslett** , a charming boutique hotel located in the heart of **Notting Hill** . This stylish yet cozy hotel offers an intimate setting with a modern British twist, perfect for couples or solo travelers who want to escape the hustle and bustle of London's more commercial areas. During Christmas, the hotel adds a touch of magic with seasonal décor and cozy rooms, making it the perfect retreat after a day of sightseeing. The neighborhood itself, known for its independent shops and charming cafes, adds to the allure of a laid-back, festive getaway.

For a more homely feel, **The Georgian House Hotel** in Pimlico offers a delightful stay in a historic townhouse. This lovely B&B provides guests with a charming atmosphere that feels like home, featuring festive touches such as a fireplace in the lounge and seasonal treats in the breakfast room. The hotel's central location means you're close to many of London's Christmas attractions, but the peaceful neighborhood ensures you'll still get a restful night's sleep.

For those who prefer to stay in a self-catering environment, **Airbnb** and **Holiday Rentals** provide countless options across London, from cozy studios to entire flats. Many of these rentals are in charming neighborhoods like **Islington** , **Camden** , or **Greenwich** , offering a more personal and homely touch to your festive stay. Many hosts will decorate their properties for the holidays, adding a personal touch to your experience. Plus, staying in a rental offers the freedom to enjoy a home-cooked Christmas meal, if you choose, with access to the local markets for fresh, seasonal produce.

Lastly, **The Franklin Hotel** in Knightsbridge is an elegant yet boutique option that combines the charm of a smaller hotel with all the luxury of the best London accommodations. The Franklin offers spacious rooms, some of which are decorated with stunning Christmas touches. Its central location, near **Harrods** and **Hyde Park** , makes it a perfect base for families or couples who want to enjoy London's Christmas markets, while the cozy interior and friendly service ensure a warm and comfortable stay.

Whether you prefer a luxurious hotel or a more intimate and charming alternative, London has a wealth of accommodation options that will make your Christmas visit unforgettable. Each place offers a unique atmosphere that enhances the city's festive charm, ensuring that your stay is filled with comfort, joy, and a touch of holiday magic.

CHAPTER 11

SHOPPING AND GIFTING GUIDE

London during the holiday season is a shopper's paradise, where festive cheer and retail therapy come together to create an unforgettable experience. The city becomes a glittering hub of holiday markets, luxurious department stores, charming boutiques, and hidden gems, all brimming with unique gifts, delightful treats, and seasonal finds. Whether you're on the hunt for a classic Christmas gift, a luxurious present for someone special, or a quirky item to surprise a friend, London's shopping scene has something for everyone.

This chapter serves as your ultimate guide to navigating the best shopping spots across the city, offering insight into the most iconic retail destinations, and helping you discover the perfect presents for every personality. From the bustling Christmas markets offering handcrafted delights to the grand department stores showcasing the latest holiday trends, there's no shortage of places to explore.

Here, we'll not only explore the top shopping destinations, but also offer expert advice on how to approach the festive shopping season, including what to look out for, where to find the most unique items, and tips for creating the most memorable gifting experience.

Get ready to immerse yourself in London's festive retail magic, as we guide you through a world of sparkling windows, holiday sales, one-of-a-kind artisan pieces, and the very best of Christmas gifting. Whether you're shopping for family, friends, colleagues, or even treating yourself, this guide will help you make the most of the London shopping experience during the most wonderful time of the year.

FINDING UNIQUE BRITISH GIFTS

London is a treasure trove of unique gifts that celebrate British heritage, craftsmanship, and the city's distinctive charm. Whether you're looking for something that embodies the elegance of the British aristocracy, the warmth of traditional craftsmanship, or a quirky piece of modern design, London offers a plethora of one-of-a-kind presents that reflect its cultural legacy.

For those seeking a truly British gift, why not start with the world-renowned British luxury brands? From the iconic trench coats of Burberry to the fine leather goods of Smythson, these items are timeless gifts that exude class and tradition. These brands, which have been part of London's fashion scene for centuries, continue to represent the very best of British style. A beautifully crafted Burberry scarf or a classic leather wallet from Smythson could make a perfect gift for someone who appreciates both style and heritage.

For a more artisanal touch, London is home to many independent stores and markets that feature handcrafted goods from local artisans. Consider stopping by Liberty, the department store housed in a Tudor-style building, where you'll find a collection of British-made goods such as pottery, glassware, and textiles. Hand-painted china from local ceramics workshops, handmade wool blankets from Scottish mills, or bespoke stationery from British printmakers make for exceptional gifts that have a personal, crafted feel.

Another great way to find unique British gifts is to visit the famous borough markets and independent shops dotted around the city. From local food producers offering rare British cheeses and chutneys to London-themed accessories, these items can be a fun and authentic way to bring a bit of London into your loved ones' lives. The charm of a quirky piece of London-inspired art or a vintage map of the city also makes for a unique, sentimental gift that beautifully captures the essence of the British capital.

11.2 CHRISTMAS SOUVENIRS AND KEEPSAKES

A visit to London during the Christmas season wouldn't be complete without taking home a souvenir that perfectly captures the magic of the holidays. From traditional decorations to handcrafted gifts, London offers a variety of keepsakes that reflect the festive spirit, making it easy to bring home a piece of the holiday magic.

One of the most popular items to collect during the Christmas season is a festive ornament. Look no further than Harrods or Hamleys for some of the finest and most luxurious Christmas decorations. These stores offer a range of high-end, beautifully crafted baubles, from traditional glass ornaments to contemporary designs.

Whether you choose a gilded London bus, a hand-painted Buckingham Palace, or a classic Christmas tree decoration, these ornaments will serve as a reminder of your time in London every holiday season.

For something a little more unique, the Christmas markets in London provide an array of charming souvenirs. Many of the festive stalls at Winter Wonderland, Southbank Centre, and Greenwich Market feature handmade products from local artisans, including knitted scarves, wood carvings, and hand-sewn stockings. These items offer not just a token of your visit, but a story of British craftsmanship. Many of these items can't be found elsewhere, making them a perfect souvenir for those seeking something truly distinctive.

Additionally, London-themed keepsakes such as miniature red phone booths, classic tea sets, or vintage postcards adorned with festive scenes of the city are always popular. The British tradition of tea is particularly strong during the winter months, so why not bring home a set of beautifully designed tea cups or a festive tin of classic English tea? These items hold a certain nostalgic quality, and they make perfect gifts for friends and family, evoking the spirit of a cozy London Christmas.

If you're looking for something a bit more personal, consider purchasing bespoke holiday gifts from London's many independent boutiques. Personalized jewelry, engraved keepsake boxes, or custom leather goods from London's artisan shops are thoughtful, one-of-a-kind gifts that beautifully capture the essence of the season. These thoughtful items reflect both the holiday spirit and London's rich cultural identity, ensuring your souvenir is more than just a trinket, but a cherished memory of your time spent in the heart of the city during the most wonderful time of the year.

CHAPTER 12

PRACTICAL TIPS FOR A SMOOTH HOLIDAY SEASON

The holiday season in London is an enchanting time, filled with festive lights, seasonal activities, and the magic of Christmas. But as much as the city sparkles with joy, navigating the hustle and bustle of this vibrant metropolis during the holidays can feel overwhelming without a little preparation. To ensure your time in London is as smooth and stress-free as possible, it's essential to plan ahead, stay organized, and keep a few practical tips in mind.

Whether you're visiting London for the first time or returning to experience its seasonal charm, this chapter is designed to guide you through the essential tips and tricks that will make your holiday experience enjoyable. From navigating the busy streets during the peak of holiday shopping to finding the best transportation options for getting around the city, we've compiled a comprehensive set of suggestions to help you make the most of your holiday visit.

Planning is key when it comes to making the most of London's festive offerings, especially with so many exciting events, attractions, and activities to choose from. This chapter provides insider advice on everything from avoiding the busiest tourist spots to ensuring you don't miss out on the most popular Christmas markets and shows. With these practical tips, you can relax and immerse yourself in the wonder of London without feeling rushed or stressed.

In addition, we'll also provide you with guidance on booking accommodations, managing holiday expenses, and preparing for London's weather during the winter months. No matter what you're hoping to experience this holiday season, these tips will empower you to navigate the city with ease, leaving you free to enjoy all the festive magic that London has to offer.

12.1

NAVIGATING LONDON DURING THE HOLIDAYS

London during the holidays is a dazzling sight, but it's also a busy, bustling city. With its festive displays, crowded shopping streets, and packed Christmas markets, it can be overwhelming if you're not prepared. The key to navigating London during the holidays is planning ahead, knowing your routes, and using public transportation efficiently. Here are some tips for making your holiday travel in London as smooth as possible:

Use Public Transportation Wisely: London has one of the most extensive public transport networks in the world, and it's your best bet for getting around during the holiday season. The London Underground (or "Tube") is the fastest way to travel across the city, but be prepared for it to be crowded, especially around central hubs like Oxford Circus and Covent Garden. To avoid the heaviest crowds, travel early in the morning or later in the evening.

Consider using **contactless payment methods** like Oyster cards or your contactless bank card to speed up your journeys. If you're planning to stay for a few days, get an Oyster card or travel pass to save money and avoid long queues.

Be Aware of Holiday Timetables: During the Christmas period, some lines or stations may operate on altered schedules, and a few may close entirely, particularly around Christmas Day and New Year's Eve. Always check online for updated schedules. Alternatively, use the **TFL Go app** for real-time transport updates and travel alerts.

Walk When You Can: London is a walkable city, and with so many of its festive attractions clustered together in central areas, walking can be a delightful way to soak in the seasonal sights. However, remember that some popular areas can get quite congested, especially shopping districts like Regent Street or Covent Garden. If you're looking to avoid the masses, take a leisurely stroll in quieter neighborhoods like Chelsea or along the South Bank.

Avoid Peak Hours: The holidays mean heavy foot traffic, particularly in tourist hotspots like Leicester Square, Covent Garden, and Oxford Street. If you're not a fan of crowds, plan your visit to these areas during off-peak times, early in the morning or later at night, when the atmosphere is still magical, but the crowds are thinner. Try to visit popular attractions like Winter Wonderland or Christmas markets during weekdays to avoid the weekend rush.

Plan for Alternative Routes: With a city this large, some routes can get clogged, particularly around major train stations like Victoria, Paddington, and King's Cross. Plan for alternative routes in advance, such as bus routes or walking paths, to avoid getting stuck in traffic or delays. The iconic red buses offer a scenic view of the city during the festive season and can often be quicker than the Tube, especially in areas with heavy foot traffic.

By taking the time to plan your transport and avoid the peak crowds, you'll be able to navigate London's festive chaos with ease and spend more time enjoying the holiday spirit rather than stressing over logistics.

12.2 STAYING SAFE AND MAKING THE MOST OF YOUR TRIP

While London during the holidays is undeniably magical, it's essential to stay safe and be mindful of a few practical considerations to make your trip as enjoyable as possible. From staying secure in crowded areas to preparing for winter weather, these tips will help you enjoy a stress-free holiday experience.

Be Weather-Ready: London winters are known for being cold, wet, and sometimes snowy, so dressing in layers is essential. Make sure to bring a warm coat, gloves, a scarf, and waterproof boots, as rain showers are common in December. Be sure to carry an umbrella, but do check the weather forecast daily, as weather conditions can change quickly. Additionally, be cautious of icy patches in pedestrian areas, especially in the mornings when sidewalks may be slippery.

Keep Your Belongings Safe: With the surge of tourists and locals heading to holiday shopping districts and markets, it's important to stay vigilant about your belongings. Pickpocketing can occur, particularly in crowded areas like Oxford Street and Leicester Square. Keep your bag zipped up and always be aware of your surroundings. A crossbody bag with a secure clasp can be more practical and safer than a backpack in these crowded spots.

Be Cautious in Crowded Places: Popular spots like Winter Wonderland, Covent Garden, and Christmas markets will draw large crowds. While the festive atmosphere is part of the charm, crowded places can be overwhelming. Keep a close eye on your personal items, and if you have young children, make sure to keep them close by. It's also a good idea to have a plan in case you get separated from your party. Make sure everyone in your group has a fully charged phone, and consider setting a meeting point in case of separation.

Stay in Well-Lit Areas: London is a relatively safe city, but it's still a good idea to stay in well-lit, populated areas after dark, especially if you're not familiar with the city. Stick to main roads and avoid quieter side streets at night. Many of London's Christmas lights, displays, and markets are best enjoyed at night, but ensure you're walking with others or in a well-traveled area for added security.

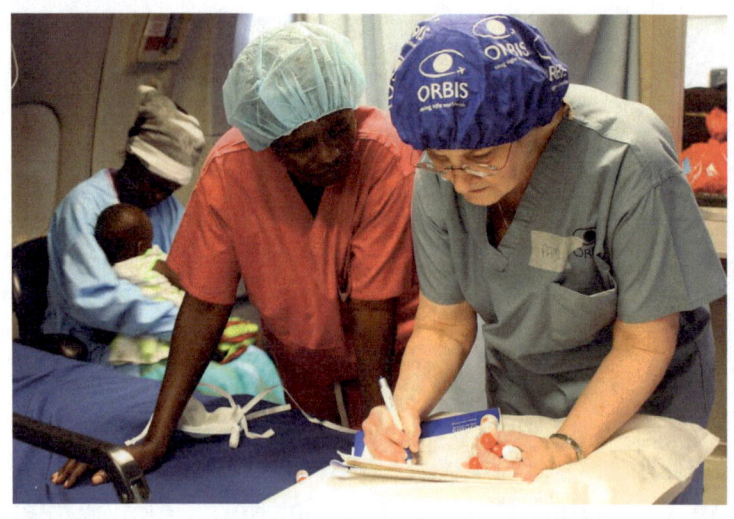

Plan for Healthcare Needs: London's healthcare services are excellent, but it's always a good idea to know where the nearest pharmacy or hospital is in case of an emergency. If you take medication or have specific health needs, be sure to bring everything you need, as finding specific medications can sometimes be challenging in a foreign city. For minor ailments, the city's many pharmacies can help with over-the-counter remedies.

Keep Your Travel Essentials Organized: If you're planning to do a lot of shopping, consider leaving your valuables in a hotel safe and only taking what you need for the day. Avoid carrying large amounts of cash, and use credit or debit cards when possible to minimize the risk of losing money.

By staying prepared for London's winter weather, being mindful of your safety in crowded areas, and keeping your essentials organized, you can make the most of the holiday season in this vibrant city.

London is a bustling, exciting destination for the holidays, and by following these practical tips, you'll be ready to experience it to the fullest, worry-free and with a sense of ease.

CONCLUSION

As we come to the close of this festive journey through London, it's clear that the magic of the holiday season truly comes alive in this vibrant city. Whether you're marveling at the twinkling lights on Oxford Street, gliding across an ice rink at Somerset House, or exploring the centuries-old traditions at Hampton Court Palace, London offers a wealth of experiences that capture the essence of Christmas. Each neighborhood, each market, and each historic site adds its own unique touch to the seasonal celebration, making it an unforgettable destination for anyone seeking the joy of the holidays.

This book has been designed to help you navigate the hustle and bustle of the season, offering detailed insights into London's best attractions, hidden gems, and practical tips for a smooth and safe experience. We've explored how to enjoy the festive spirit without feeling overwhelmed, from shopping for one-of-a-kind gifts to finding cozy accommodations that perfectly match the holiday atmosphere. Whether you're visiting with family, friends, or venturing out on your own, London has something to offer for everyone, from the traditional to the contemporary.

As you prepare for your holiday in this magnificent city, remember that the heart of the experience lies not only in the sights and activities but also in the simple moments of joy—the laughter of children skating on the ice, the warmth of a holiday drink shared with loved ones, and the sense of wonder that fills the air as you stroll past the festive displays. London is more than a destination; it's an invitation to create lasting memories, embrace new traditions, and soak in the beauty of the season.

So, as you embark on your London holiday, take with you the knowledge, tips, and insights you've gathered here. Plan ahead, explore with open eyes, and let the city's festive spirit sweep you away. Whether it's your first time visiting or you're returning to experience London's holiday magic once again, there's no better place to make the most of this special time of year.

Thank you for joining me on this holiday adventure, and may your Christmas in London be filled with warmth, wonder, and the joy of the season.

Made in United States
Troutdale, OR
11/21/2024

25133846R10071